Building History
INDUS VALLEY CITY

Gillian Clements

W
FRANKLIN WATTS
LONDON • SYDNEY

First published in 2004 by
Franklin Watts
96 Leonard Street
London
EC2A 4XD

Franklin Watts Australia
45-51 Huntley Street
Alexandria
NSW 2015

© Gillian Clements 2004

Editor: Sally Luck
Art Director: Jonathan Hair
Consultant: Dr Justin Morris,
   Curator of South Asian Archaeology,
   The British Museum, London

ISBN: 0 7496 5140 7

A CIP catalogue record for this book is
available from the British Library.

Printed in Malaysia

Contents

What was an Indus Valley city?

Four-and-a-half thousand years ago, a civilisation flourished in the valley surrounding the Indus River, in Southern Asia. It was the ancient world's largest civilisation but, until recently, it remained undiscovered – buried under the ground.

What is a civilisation?

The word 'civilisation' refers to a large, organised group of people with a shared culture. Unlike most people who lived thousands of years ago, the Indus people were not travelling hunters. They came together to live in villages, towns and cities, with laws and rules; they formed a civilisation.

Where were the Indus cities?

In the 1920s, archaeologists were digging in the Indus Valley in North-west India (in an area which later became Pakistan). They discovered two remarkable cities, Mohenjo-daro and Harappa. The two cities were a long way apart - 563 km - but were very alike. Both had a higher, walled area (called a citadel) and a lower area beneath, with hundreds of houses.

EUROPE

AFRICA

Mediterranean Sea

GREECE

Black Sea

Caspian Sea

Euphrates River

Tigris River

ASIA

Approximate boundary of the Indus civilisation

Himalayan Mountains

Harappa

Mohenjo-daro

Indus River

EGYPT

Nile River

ARABIA

Arabian Sea

The Indus civilisation covered over a million square kilometres of land. That's four times the size of the United Kingdom!

3300BC	3300-2800BC	2600-2500BC	1900-1700BC
Mohenjo-daro and Harappa are riverside farming villages.	People farming in the area begin to form larger settlements.	Indus civilisation grows and spreads. Craftsmanship and trade help towns and cities develop.	The Indus civilisation ends. Small local cultures replace it.

When did the civilisation flourish?

The Indus civilisation began around 2600BC. At this time, people in the Indus area began making a new kind of pottery and started a new religion. These changes helped bring about the rise and success of the Indus civilisation. In the centuries between 2600 and 1900BC the culture grew, flourished and then seemed to disappear.

Indus ▶ jewellery, pottery and seals

Where did the Indus people live?

Many people lived in the Indus cities. However, thousands more lived in villages and towns around the Indus River, and other important rivers. Some people lived in trading out-posts, south at the coast or north in the foothills of the Himalayan Mountains. These settlements were a long way from the cities and were used by travelling traders.

An Indus priest

An area of houses inside an Indus Valley city ▶

Who built the cities?

The evidence found by archaeologists suggests that religious leaders or merchants planned the layout of the cities. They would then have organised villagers and townspeople into gangs of labourers to carry out the building work.

7

Who discovered the Indus cities?

Some local Indian legends told of an ancient city in the Punjab district. However, few people realised that there was a great civilisation beneath their feet! Sir Alexander Cunningham was the first archaeologist to excavate the area.

Sir Alexander Cunningham was an important British archaeologist working in India at the end of the 19th century, when India was part of the British Empire. When local people from the Harappa area found strange brick ruins, Cunningham thought they were only a few years old and probably from a Buddhist temple. However, in his first Harappa excavation (1872-73) he found no temples – just pottery, and a mysterious stamp seal.

British people living in India considered some parts of the country to be wild and uncivilised. They did not believe that a complex civilisation had existed in the Punjab, thousands of years before. They were wrong!

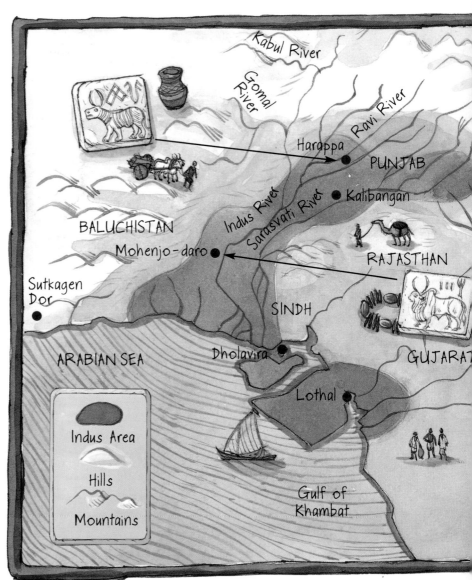

Sir John Marshall was the British director of the Archaeological Survey of India in the 1920s. In 1924, his excavations revealed a huge citadel platform at Mohenjo-daro. He then announced the discovery of the unknown Indus civilisation!

Rakal Das Banerji was the Superintending Archaeologist of the Western Circle. He excavated in 1919 and found Indus seals.

Bahadur Daya Ram Sahni excavated at Harappa in 1920 and 1921. He found more seals with different words and pictures.

George Dales & Mark Kenoyer excavated Harappa in 1986 and discovered more about Indus craftsmen and merchants.

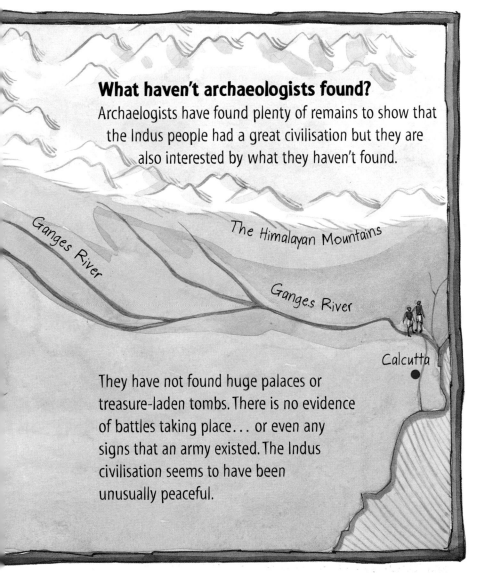

What haven't archaeologists found?

Archaelogists have found plenty of remains to show that the Indus people had a great civilisation but they are also interested by what they haven't found.

Ganges River

The Himalayan Mountains

Ganges River

Calcutta

They have not found huge palaces or treasure-laden tombs. There is no evidence of battles taking place… or even any signs that an army existed. The Indus civilisation seems to have been unusually peaceful.

How do archaelogists find out about the past?

Archaeologists often have to dig through layers in the ground to find out about the past. Each layer represents a 'living surface', on which people have lived and built their homes. After many years, buildings fall down and the ground flattens. Each time this happens, new homes are built and the 'living surface' level becomes higher. Archaeologists can date each level by identifying the buildings, pottery, coins and other artefacts that they find there.

▲ Diagram showing 'living surface' layers

Archaeological work has continued in the Indus area ever since the first big excavations.

Why build near a river?

Harappa, the great city of the Upper Indus region, was built next to the Ravi River. Mohenjo-daro, in the Lower Indus region, was on the right bank of the Indus. There were many reasons for building near a river.

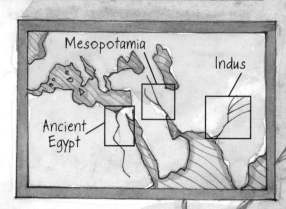

Water for ceremonies

The Great Bath, in Mohenjo-daro's citadel, was probably used for worshippers to clean themselves during religious ceremonies. It had to be built near a river to get a good supply of water.

In the 1970s, it was discovered that there were as many settlements along the sacred Sarasvati River as there were along the Indus. For this reason, the civilisation is sometimes called the Indus-Sarasvati civilisation.

Ganweriwala

INDUS RIVER

Mohenjo-daro

Chanhu-daro

Water for farming

The Indus River was at its lowest level in winter and highest in mid-summer. Barley and wheat were sown just after the mid-summer floods and they grew well, even without ploughing and irrigation. Other crops needed river irrigation.

Sofka Koh

Dholavira

ARABIAN SEA

River trade and communications

Trade was very important to the huge Indus culture. Bullock carts made good overland vehicles, if the land was flat. However, travelling by river and sea was the fastest and easiest way to take goods to faraway markets.

RAVI RIVER

Harappa

Kalibangan

SARASVATI RIVER

Water supply and waste disposal

Keeping cities clean was very important to the Indus people. Waste water in city drains and sewers was channelled away from the cities, out towards the rivers. There was also a good supply of water to public and private wells.

Fishing

Indus people ate a lot of fish. They fished for carp in the rivers and for a variety of fish in the sea. Living near a river gave people a good food supply.

Were other civilisations built on rivers?

Nile River

EGYPT

Egypt

Ancient Egypt's civilisation grew up along the River Nile, where the land was fertile for farming. Cities, towns and the famous pyramids were built along its banks, and builders and traders relied on it to transport stone and goods.

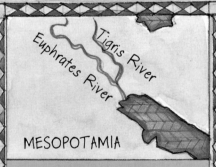

Tigris River

Euphrates River

MESOPOTAMIA

Mesopotamia

This area is sometimes called 'the cradle of civilisation', as it is where the first cities were built. The land between the Tigris and Euphrates rivers was fertile and good for farming. The area became home to the ancient Sumerian and Assyrian cultures.

11

Who were the Indus people?

It is difficult for us to find out a lot about the Indus people, because we can't understand their writing. We have to look at archaeological evidence to try to learn about them.

What did they look like?

Hairstyles

Stone and clay Indus sculptures show us that men had a variety of hairstyles. Some women had simple braids but others had intricate hairstyles, or wore hats. Their clothes varied too, and this probably depended on their job or their place in society.

Indus sculptures ▼

The famous 'Priest King' sculpture ▲

An Indus farmer ▲

Jewellery

Indus people wore a lot of jewellery, such as bangles and necklaces. Craftsmen were skilled at making beads from different kinds of stone. As with clothing, the type of jewellery people wore may have shown their place in society.

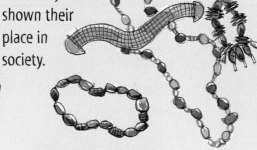

What did they believe?

Water ceremonies

The cleanliness of the cities and the Great Bath of Mohenjo-daro suggest that water was an important part of Indus religion. Water is also very important in Hinduism, one of the major religions in India today.

Shells, used as water vessels in ceremonies

Burials

In the grave sites at Harappa, Lothal and Kalibangan, bodies have been found buried with pottery and other personal items. This suggests that Indus people believed in an afterlife which, again, probably linked into religious beliefs.

Pottery found in graves ▲

◄ This seal might show a marriage procession of the gods.

Religious seals

Many Indus seals show pictures of gods, which indicates how important religion was to them. Plants, trees and animals also feature. These are important in the Hindu religion today and many archaeologists believe elements of this may link back to the Indus culture (see pages 24-25).

What did the Indus people do?

Farmers grew a great variety of crops such as barley, wheat, rice, chickpeas, field peas, mustard, sesame, grapes, dates, melon and cotton. They also raised animals such as cattle, water buffalo, sheep, goats, pigs, chickens, dogs and camels.

Traders used seals to identify their trade goods. Many Indus people were traders. Seals from the Indus Valley have been found as far away as Mesopotamia, Central Asia, Iran and Afghanistan. This tells us that traders travelled far to sell their goods.

Craftsmen made things for people to use in their homes, such as pottery and tools. These goods were also traded, as were luxury items. Gemstones, such as cornelian and lapis lazuli, became beautiful beaded jewellery in the skilled hands of the Indus craftsmen.

Priests played an important part in ruling the civilisation. There would probably have been a major priest in each town or city, who acted as a local ruler. Other priests may have collected goods from the public, both for taxes and for making offerings to the gods.

Women The clay and stone figurines show us what women might have looked like, but we can only guess at what their daily activities were. Women were most probably involved in running the household, but could they have had jobs outside the home too?

Why did their cities grow?

The Indus cities grew for two main reasons; the people had clever business minds, and there were excellent river, coastal and overland trade routes.

Area in which Indus people travelled to trade

How did trade routes help the cities grow?

Traders and craftsmen used the trade routes to bring raw materials (from the Indus area and further afield) into the towns and cities, where they were turned into jewellery, pottery and metalware. Such goods were very valuable and helped the cities to prosper and grow.

WEST:
Indus traders travelled to Mesopotamia and Persia by land and, more usually, by sea.

How did the Indus traders travel around?

Long, flat-bottomed ferry-boats were used to carry people and goods by river. However, to travel to places like Mesopotamia and Persia (modern Iran), it was quicker to sail in strong sea boats up the Persian Gulf. On land, Indus traders used bullock carts.

Did the Indus people trade in Mesopotamia?

The Mesopotamians wrote about importing goods from the Indus people. Their texts mention gold, copper, lapis lazuli and wood. The fact that archaeologists have found Indus seals and other artefacts in Mesopotamia proves that Indus people traded there.

NORTH:
Indus traders travelled north as far as Central Asia looking for jade to make jewellery. Nearer to the Indus area, in Afghanistan, they bought gold and lapis lazuli.

	Major trade routes
	Cornelian
	Timber
	Shell
	Fish
	Copper
	Gold
	Silver
	Flint
	Steatite
	Turquoise
	Amethyst
	Alabaster
	Jade
	Lapis lazuli

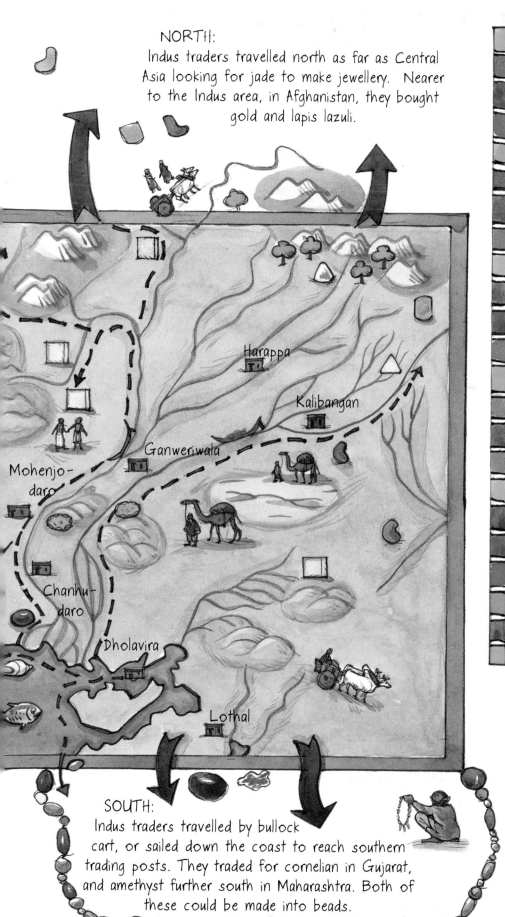

Harappa

Kalibangan

Ganweriwala

Mohenjo-daro

Chanhu-daro

Dholavira

Lothal

SOUTH:
Indus traders travelled by bullock cart, or sailed down the coast to reach southern trading posts. They traded for cornelian in Gujarat, and amethyst further south in Maharashtra. Both of these could be made into beads.

It is hard to work out how many people lived in each of the Indus cities. Some historians think that, at its largest, Harappa's population was as much as 80,000!

How was an Indus city planned?

When archaeologists excavated mysterious brick and earth mounds around the Indus area, they found rectangular cities and towns, laid out in an orderly grid pattern.

This map shows the excavation site at Mohenjo-daro, as found by Marshall's team (see page 8)

The citadel and the lower city

Big Indus cities like Mohenjo-daro and Harappa had two main parts: a high-walled citadel to the west and a lower city to the east. At Mohenjo-daro, archaeologists discovered a street grid dividing the city into 12 blocks of houses.

The area of the Mohenjo-daro citadel

Great Bath

Granary

College

Pillared hall

Remains of citadel wall

Mohenjo-daro's citadel

The citadel was surrounded by six-metre high walls and had mostly civic and religious buildings inside. Some religious leaders may have lived there too. To enter the sacred area, visitors had to climb a tall flight of stairs and pass through a bathing place where they may have had to wash to purify themselves.

Like the Egyptians, Indus people used their knowledge of the heavens to find true north. From that, they were able to line up their city streets north-south, east-west.

The North Star!

Were the granaries really granaries?

For a long time, experts thought that hall-like buildings in citadels were granaries, for storing grain. These buildings were built on blocks to allow the air to flow underneath, just like the ancient Roman granaries. However, no traces of grain have been found and archaeologists now wonder if these granaries were actually palaces!

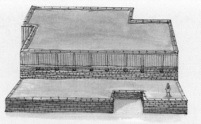

The granary at Mohenjo-daro

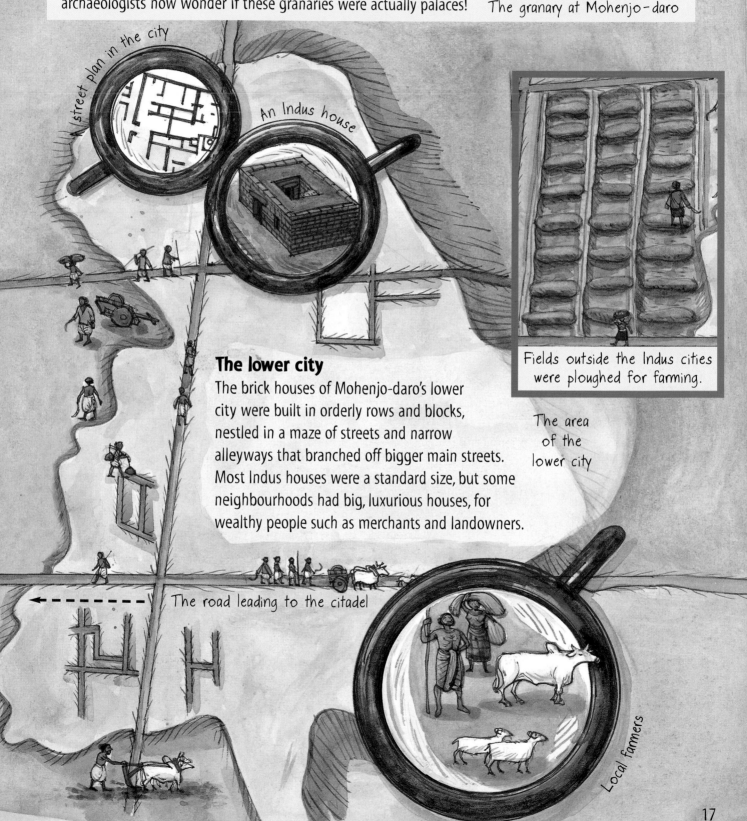

A street plan in the city

An Indus house

The lower city

The brick houses of Mohenjo-daro's lower city were built in orderly rows and blocks, nestled in a maze of streets and narrow alleyways that branched off bigger main streets. Most Indus houses were a standard size, but some neighbourhoods had big, luxurious houses, for wealthy people such as merchants and landowners.

Fields outside the Indus cities were ploughed for farming.

The area of the lower city

The road leading to the citadel

Local farmers

How did they build the cities?

Builders used materials that they found locally. Most bricks were made from mud, which was easy to find all along the riverbanks!

Brick-making was a very important industry. Huge quantities of bricks were needed for the Indus cities.

Builders used brick instead of stone, because local stone was hard to find.

They used timber to strengthen big brick structures, like the walls of the citadel.

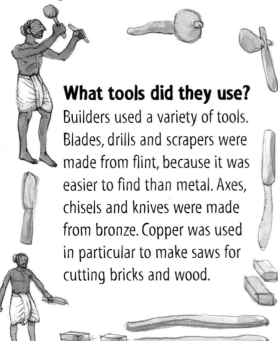

What tools did they use?

Builders used a variety of tools. Blades, drills and scrapers were made from flint, because it was easier to find than metal. Axes, chisels and knives were made from bronze. Copper was used in particular to make saws for cutting bricks and wood.

How did they make the bricks?

Brick-makers made most of their bricks to a standard size. The uniform size and shape made Indus city walls and buildings look really impressive!

Brick-makers filled wooden moulds with mud, and left them to dry out.

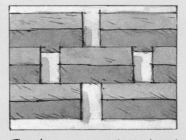

The bricks were tipped out of their moulds and stacked.

Bricks were baked hard in the Sun or in an oven for extra strength.

A few bricks were sawn to a particular size.

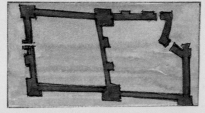

Citadel walls were often many metres thick.

The bricks were laid in a special 'bond' which made a long and short pattern.

How did they build the Great Bath?

Builders had to make the base and sides of the Bath completely watertight. They did this by sandwiching a substance called bitumen tar between layers of specially sawn bricks. When the builders had finished building the Bath, they built raised columns on the Bath's north, east and south sides.

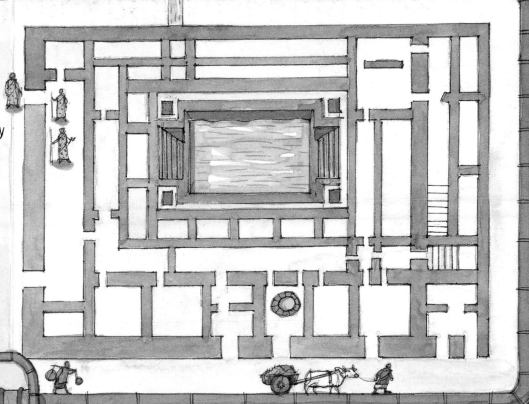

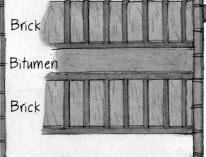

Brick

Bitumen

Brick

How was the Great Bath supplied with water?

A large well supplied the Great Bath with water. The water could then be drained through a corner outlet into a bigger drain, and away out of the city.

In all the Indus cities, the standard size of brick was 7 cm x 14 cm x 28 cm (a ratio of 1:2:4).

A brick alleyway in the lower city

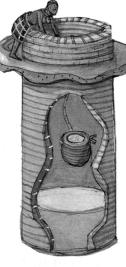

Cross-section of a well

How did they control the city's water?

Indus cities had public and private wells, and drains from all the lower city's houses. These fed into street drains, and then into even bigger drains which ran along the centre of most main streets.

What was city life like?

The Indus cities would have been peaceful places to live, controlled by priests, merchants and landowners.

How did religion affect city life?

Religious ceremonies were a big part of city life and they normally took place in the citadels. Priests may have held sacred bathing ceremonies at the Great Bath at Mohenjo-daro. Not far away archaeologists have found a statue lying in an oblong, colonnaded building. This is thought to have been a temple for religious worship.

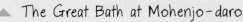

▲ The Great Bath at Mohenjo-daro   ▲ The granary at Mohenjo-daro

How did traders pass in and out of the city?

Most Indus cities had carefully located entrances in the thick walls. Some were narrow but others were wide enough for a bullock cart to pass through. As traders passed in and out, city officials may have taxed them and their goods. They would have used stone seals pressed into clay tabs to mark the goods.

The distinctive Indus seals were pressed into wet clay, to form clay tabs. They left a raised impression – normally of some writing with a picture below.

What happened in the lower city?

Most people lived in the lower city, east of the citadel. Archaeologists have found Indus homes and workshops side by side here. The homes came in different sizes. This shows that there were probably different layers of society: the rich and the not so rich!

What happened in the craft workshops?

Craftsmen made seals from grey steatite stone. They were cut and carved with a copper tool.

Making etched cornelian and long-barrelled beads required great skill. Beads were also made from materials such as clay, stone, shell and ivory.

Archaeologists have found cotton bags and cotton fishing lines. Raw cotton bales must have been spun, woven and dyed in the lower city.

Clay was used to make different kinds of pottery. Some pots were made to hold seals, beads and jewellery.

Most pots were made on pottery wheels, then fired (baked) and decorated with red slip (runny clay) and black patterns.

Death in the city

Indus people were buried with personal items which suggests that they believed in an afterlife. However, they weren't wasteful people and they didn't bury precious items with their dead.

Experts have studied the bones of people buried in the cities. They can tell that, in life, these people were well-fed and healthy. Poorer people may have been cremated or have had river burials.

What was it like inside a house?

The Indus mud-brick city houses had high ceilings and thick walls, to keep them cool in the heat of the day. Some houses had just one room, with a bathing area partitioned off. But rich people had large homes with several rooms, a courtyard and an upper floor.

Householders could relax in the Sun on a brick platform outside the house, or work in the shade of a tree.

The kitchen had a hearth, and was in one of the outer rooms.

This fish looks tasty!

Windows let in light and air. Some may have had wooden or stone lattice grilles, and wooden shutters.

The living room may have been used as a workshop, where beads, stone tools, pots and other domestic artefacts were made.

People entered their homes from a side lane. Walls next to the main streets had no doors or windows, for peace and privacy.

See you at lunch time!

The city was kept litter-free. Workmen cleared rubbish from bins built on the sides of houses.

22

The upper floor was used for stores and for personal rooms.

Did people work in their homes?

Experts think that some people had workshop areas in their home – in the courtyard or in the living room. However, they have also found buildings which seem like separate workshops. These were in the same part of town as the houses.

The flat roof was made using strong wooden beams, filled in with matting and plaster. People worked, relaxed and slept there in the open air.

How were the houses supplied with water?

Many city homes had private wells, latrines and bathrooms. The best bathrooms had watertight brickwork on the floors and in the drains. The water system was very efficient for its time. Open waste drains led out through pipes and chutes to street drains – and eventually to city sewers.

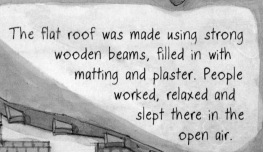

Waste water drained into the sewer.

The well

Brick stairs led to upstairs rooms and the flat roof.

The courtyard was a quiet place for work (including weaving and washing clothes) and for relaxation. Children could play there in safety.

How has the Indus culture continued?

The Indus people may have lived as far back as 2800BC. However, some aspects of their culture have survived and are still part of life in India and Pakistan today.

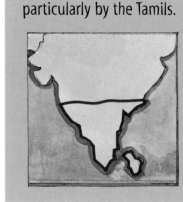

Religion

Indus seals often have pictures of bulls, tigers, elephants, tree-spirits and of gods who are seated cross-legged. In fact Indus people and modern-day Hindus seem to share some gods and goddesses, and honour the same animals and trees.

This Indus seal shows an elephant. Hindus worship the elephant god, Ganesha.

The cow and bull

The cow and bull are sacred to Hindus, as symbols of fertility and prosperity. Historians believe they were sacred to the Indus people, possibly for the same reasons.

The area where the Indus people lived is now largely Muslim. However, it is the Hindu religion that has carried forward some of the Indus culture.

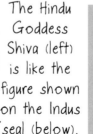

The Hindu Goddess Shiva (left) is like the figure shown on the Indus seal (below).

Script and language

Experts believe that the Dravidian language of the Indus people is similar to the one spoken today in the south of India, particularly by the Tamils.

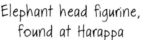
◀ Elephant head figurine, found at Harappa

Society

Indus and Indian society seem to share a class or caste system. The high-class Indian Brahmins (the priestly caste) may be like a modern Hindu version of the ancient Indus priest-rulers.

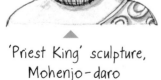

'Priest King' sculpture, Mohenjo-daro

Cleanliness and bathing

The idea of purification, which was so important to the Indus people, continues in the modern Hindu religion. One of the most sacred pilgrimages Hindus make is to bathe in the Ganges River.

Bathing at the Ganges

Jewellery

Modern Hindu bangles, necklaces and nose ornaments look very like ancient Indus jewellery. Bangles are a particularly important way of showing a woman's status.

Boats

Local Pakistanis on the Indus River still use flat-bottomed ferry-boats for their main river transport, just like their ancestors did.

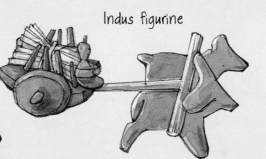

Indus seal

boat today

Bullock carts

Bullock carts are still used today near Mohenjo-daro. The modern designs sometimes include framed covers.

Indus figurine

cart today

Farming

Farmers use terracing to farm the hills around Islamabad in Pakistan, much as the ancient Indus farmers did. Many Indus crops and animals are still grown and raised by modern farmers in the area.

What happened to the Indus cities?

The Indus civilisation fell into decay and collapsed in the centuries between 1900 and 1700 BC.
A number of things might have caused this... but no one knows for sure what it was.

Could the Indus rivers have destroyed the civilisation?

In the Indus area, rivers sometimes change their course and either dry up or flood. Such changes could have made farming impossible and caused major food shortages. There is evidence that Mohenjo-daro experienced several floods. Could there have been one huge flood which finally destroyed the city?

Could there have been an invasion?

In India's *Rig Veda* hymns (Hindu poems dating from about 1500 BC) there is mention of Aryan tribes destroying Indus cities. However, excavations don't back this story up because there is no evidence of widespread destruction. Also, the timing for the invasion mentioned in the hymns is wrong.

Were there earthquakes in the area?

Earthquakes could have caused flooding in parts of the Indus Valley, and destroyed Mohenjo-daro.

Mosquito

Could disease have ruined Indus city life?

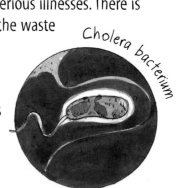

Archaeologists studying the skeletons at the Mohenjo-daro site have discovered that many people died from malaria, carried by mosquitoes, and other serious illnesses. There is even a suggestion that the waste from the city drains contaminated the well water and caused an outbreak of cholera. This would have killed a lot of people and perhaps made it impossible for others to survive.

Cholera bacterium

What do we know about life outside the cities?

Most Indus people were farmers who lived in rural areas. However, very little research has been done to find out what life outside the cities was like. Some of the surviving clay figurines are of rural people, and some villages and herdsmen's camps have been found, but this is the only evidence which has been analysed. Work is now planned to find out more about the farming population.

Recently, a team of historians suspended a camera on a specially designed hot-air balloon which they floated over the Mohenjo-daro site. The camera took hundreds of aerial photographs which record all the remains in the city.

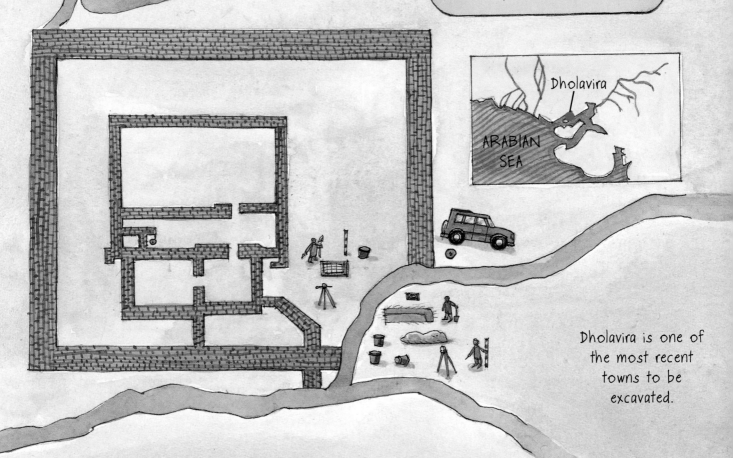

Dholavira

ARABIAN SEA

Dholavira is one of the most recent towns to be excavated.

What can we hope to find out in the future?

Since the big excavations in the 1920s, technology has advanced considerably. Work is being done today, with the most up-to-date techniques and equipment, to re-assess the findings of past excavations. Through this work, and through new excavation work at other 'town sites' and rural areas, archaeologists hope to be able to answer some of the remaining questions, such as who ruled the civilisation, how did they rule a huge area without an army, and what caused the collapse of the magnificent Indus civilisation?

Timeline

 6500-4000BC Simple farming in what today is North-west India and Pakistan. People use stone, copper and bronze.

 4000-3300 More farming settlements appear in the Indus area. They produce copper metalwork, fired wheel pottery and beadwork.

 3300 Harappa is a farming village near the Ravi River. Mohenjo-daro is a village on the Indus.

 2800 Indus people begin to develop their own form of writing.

 2600-2500 The full Indus civilisation begins. It is a time of rapid change when craftsmanship and trade help the towns and cities to develop.

 2600-1900 The Indus civilisation is at its height. There is city planning, writing, and trade with Mesopotamia.

 2200 Harappa covers 370 acres. There were possibly as many as 80,000 people living there.

 1900-1700 Trade and farming decline in the Indus area. Local cultures emerge. By 1600 the Indus culture reaches its end and is forgotten.

 c. AD 1700 The British begin to rule India. Their colonial rule lasts until Indian independence, in 1947.

 1800s The first Indus stamp seals are found but are not identified as part of an ancient civilisation.

 1920-21 The first excavations in Harappa and Mohenjo-daro take place, led by Sir John Marshall.

 1948 Archaeologist Sir Mortimer Wheeler excavates and finds early Indus pottery.

 1986 Pakistanis and Americans carry out major digs in Harappa. They realise its population is far larger than previous estimates.

 Today teams of international archaeologists continue to excavate at Harappa, Dholavira and elsewhere.

Glossary

archaeologist
A person who digs up and studies the remains of buildings and objects from the past to find out about the people who made them.

artefacts
An object made by humans, such as a tool or a dish. The word is often used to describe objects of historical interest.

bitumen tar
A black, sticky, oil-based mud, found naturally in some areas. In Indus times, it was used to seal bricks together to make watertight buildings and wells.

citadel
An important area of a city, protected by walls. In Indus cities, the citadel is on a raised platform and contains religious and civic buildings. Unlike citadels in other parts of the world, Indus citadels do not seem to have been built to give people a safe place to hide if their city came under attack.

civic
If something is civic it is to do with a town or a city. For example, a town hall is a civic building.

excavate
To dig up an area of land in order to search for historical remains. An **excavation** is an archaeological dig.

flint
A very hard stone that was often used in the past to make tools, such as axes and knives.

granary
Large building used for storing grain.

hearth
The floor of a fireplace, or a type of fireplace that is not built into a wall.

merchant
Someone who buys and sells or trades things. A merchant can also be called a trader.

seal
A small stone with a picture or writing carved on it. A seal is pushed into something soft, like clay or wax, to stamp the picture or writing into it. Seals were used in Indus times, mainly to record the buying and selling of goods.

trade routes
Pathways and roads used by traders and merchants to travel across land or water to sell their goods.

Index